PROFESSIONAL
faux
finishes
made easy

PATRICK DALY

NORTH LIGHT BOOKS
CINCINNATI, OHIO
www.artistsnetwork.com

Other fine North Light Books are available from your local bookstore or art supply store, or direct from the publisher.

09 08 07 06 05   5 4 3 2 1

Distributed in Canada by Fraser Direct
100 Armstrong Avenue
Georgetown, ON, Canada L7G 5S4
Tel: (905) 877-4411

Distributed in the U.K. and Europe by David & Charles
Brunel House, Newton Abbot, Devon, TQ12 4PU, England
Tel: (+44) 1626 323200, Fax: (+44) 1626 323319
Email: mail@davidandcharles.co.uk

Distributed in Australia by Capricorn Link
P.O. Box 704, S. Windsor, NSW 2756 Australia
Tel: (02) 4577-3555

Library of Congress Cataloging-in-Publication Data
Daly, Patrick
    Professional faux finishes made easy / Patrick Daly.
        p. cm.
    Includes index.
    ISBN 1-58180-601-9 (pbk. : alk. paper)
    1. House painting. 2. Texture painting. 3. Finishes and finishing. 4. Interior decoration. I. Title.
    TT323.D35 2005
    698'.1--dc22

                          2004029567

Editor: Christina D. Read
Designer: Clare Finney
Production Coordinator: Kristen D. Heller
Photographers: Tim Grondin, Weronica Ankarörn, Andrea VanKirk
Additional photographs supplied by: Anne Soulé, Everett & Soulé

Metric Conversion Chart		
to convert	to	multiply by
Inches	Centimeters	2.54
Centimeters	Inches	0.4
Feet	Centimeters	30.5
Centimeters	Feet	0.03
Yards	Meters	0.9
Meters	Yards	1.1
Sq. Inches	Sq. Centimeters	6.45
Sq. Centimeters	Sq. Inches	0.16
Sq. Feet	Sq. Meters	0.09
Sq. Meters	Sq. Feet	10.8
Sq. Yards	Sq. Meters	0.8
Sq. Meters	Sq. Yards	1.2
Pounds	Kilograms	0.45
Kilograms	Pounds	2.2
Ounces	Grams	28.3
Grams	Ounces	0.035

DEDICATION

I would like to dedicate this book to my children, Sterling Austin Daly, age 10, and Greyson Zane Daly, age 3. You are my inspiration and I hope to make you proud. I love you— Daddy

Donna Dewberry & Patrick Daly

ABOUT THE ARTIST

Patrick Daly is a renowned faux finish artist and instructor. Patrick has decorated many elite homes across the nation. Some of these homes have been photographed and featured in magazines such as *Architectural Digest*, *House Beautiful*, *Orlando Magazine* and *Florida Design Magazine*.

When Donna Dewberry met Patrick, she immediately recognized the wealth of knowledge, talent and experience that he had to share and invited him to develop an education program through Dewberry Designs.

ACKNOWLEDGMENTS

I would like to start by thanking Marc and Donna Dewberry. I met them through a mutual friend and since meeting them, I have found two very special friends.

There are so many people that have helped me over the years, both professionally and personally. I feel so much gratitude for them, so I would like to recognize them here. Mom and Dad, I love you. Thank you to Donald & Sylvia Stearn, Star Scenic Supply, Ray & Jan Coudriet, Morgan Luton—for always being there to help, Mark Nasrallah, Lori Paulucci, Everett & Soulé Photography, Peter S. Cahall/Newport Group, Marc Michaels Interior Design, Design Specifications Inc., Shaquille O'Neal, Tamia & Grant Hill, Horace Grant, Wesley Snipes, Payne Hughes, Stephanie Paprosky, Marc Thee, Michael Abbott, Laura Anistasia, Beth Keller, Sister Lucey Vasquez, Lulu Stevens, Kelley McCoy, Rob & Cindy Theisen, Todd & Natasha Woodbridge, Ralph & Vicki Kuhn, Mike & Patty Stokes, Suzen Ettenger, Daniel Daly, Mark & Shaney Daly, Mike & Lu Daly, Chris & Michelle Daly, Althea Credland, photographers Tim Grondin, Weronica Ankarörn and Andrea VanKirk, and my editor, Chris Read.

To anyone that I have forgotten, please know I appreciate you so much. I have truly been blessed!

Contents

Introduction

FAUX FINISHING started out as a hobby, but it was always something I was passionate about. I got my start when I met Angela Brooks through a friend. Angela asked me if I knew how to faux finish and I told her that I did (even though I didn't). She showed me some of the techniques she knew, and my faux finishing career started then. Angela and I worked as faux finishers together, before she went into a career as an interior designer. I learned by trial and error. With a lot of practice, I was able to perfect my craft.

My work has given me the opportunity to travel throughout the country. I've worked with celebrities and people in middle America. And when I wasn't working, I had the chance to see a lot of places I probably would never have visited. Traveling and the interaction with so many wonderful people are a great part of my career.

I love the fact that I can make a living by doing something I truly enjoy. And it is a privilege to work in people's homes and earn their trust—you can't put a monetary value on that! This has brought much joy into my life, and I am so grateful for the opportunity to create this book.

The technique featured on these walls, Rub & Run, is so simple, yet it infuses the room with a quiet elegance. However, the real beauty of this technique is its ease of application.

Photo courtesy of Anne Soulé, Everett & Soulé

Materials

Some of the tools of the trade:
bucket for mixing, glaze and
Venetian plaster

PAINT

I found a paint called Breakthrough that is perfect for any project and is made from a very old technology. It acts as both the primer and the paint and comes in either a satin or gloss finish or as a clear coat in satin or gloss finish.

Another great product is Artist's Choice Saturated Paints. This line of paint products can be mixed with other latex paint or varnishes and can even be mixed into a white primer. It can be used on walls, wood, metal or glass. It's a latex (water-based) paint.

As for specialty paints, I like Chromatone Quick Dry Latex Metallics. This is a ready-made metallic that comes in various colors and is sold in different sizes—from pints to gallons. I like to use this product for stenciling. It also adds a touch of understated elegance to wrought iron.

GLAZES

Nu-Glaze Glazing Liquid is a heavy-bodied pigmented glaze. It's great for woodgraining, aging (especially on gilded surfaces), antiquing and adding depth to a finish. This is an oil-based product. It has a long open time.

I also use Golden Artist Colors glazes, especially the Taupe and Metallic Bronze glazes. This is an acrylic water-based product. I use it for stenciling, color washes, sponging, ragging, stippling and marbling.

PLASTER

Kolcaustico Venetian Plaster is the brand I use most often. This plaster comes ready to use in pure white. Then the plaster can be tinted to any color. This is a thin-bodied plaster and can be a little messy. It takes some practice to get used to the consistency. This plaster is applied with plastering blades. Make sure to apply it in thin layers; the more layers, the better to create depth.

I also use Smoothrock Pearls & Metals acrylic plaster. This is a plaster much like Venetian plaster except it can be purchased already tinted or as a neutral base. It is a thicker plaster and is great to use on rough-surfaced walls.

1. soft artist brush 2. round mop brush 3. Badger softening brush 4. no. 6 round brush 5. sea sponge 6. 2-inch (51mm) paint brush/chip brush 7. artist brush 8. ½-inch (13mm) angle brush 9. 1-inch (25mm) flat brush 10. flogger brush 11. fitch brush 12. small softening brush 13. Venetian plaster blades 14. terry cloth pad 15. graining tool 16. stiff-bristled brush 17. 4-inch (10cm) brush

WAXES

Liberon Black Bison Fine Paste Wax is a fine furniture wax. The colors I usually use are Stripped Pine, Walnut, Tudor Oak, Victorian Mahogany and Teak. Waxing is the final step after plastering. It is applied by blade or rag and then buffed till the walls have a distinct sheen. I'm always asked if waxed walls can be eventually painted over. The solution is to take mineral spirits and wipe down the wall, let it dry, then replaster or paint.

BLADES

These blades are not your normal drywall tools. They are used for plaster, not drywall.

Venetian plaster is very thin, so load your blade with less than 1-inch (3cm) of plaster, at the end of the blade. Hold the blade in the palm of your hand. No pressure is needed; you are applying plaster in the same manner as icing a cake. Make sure to work small sections at a time. There may be some visible lines when you are finished.

Plaster blades come in different sizes; make sure to change blade sizes with every layer of plaster. Of course, the size of the blade should fit the size of the work space. To keep the blade from rusting, clean off the plaster by spraying some WD-40 on the blade.

BRUSHES

When I started my career, I could not afford the brushes I use today. But learning with less expensive brushes made me a better artist. I love brushes and have many of them. I use them for latex and oil materials. It's important to immediately clean them thoroughly when you are finished using them. I use a brush and roller cleaner. Soak the brushes, then use a wire brush to comb through the brushes. Be good to your brushes and they'll be good to you.

I use softening brushes quite a bit, especially when gilding and graining. I clean them out with mineral spirits, then use shampoo and conditioner, since they are made from natural materials.

SPONGES & SPONGE ROLLERS

All sponges are not created equal. I have painted with three of the same sponges for the last ten years. I have about twenty sponges and I use different ones for their imprints.

I use sponges to create leather, stone and marble effects and a verdi patina on iron gates. They are also used to soften base colors or glazes. Always be consistent in the space you paint.

When I have a large ceiling area to work on, I use the sponge roller. If I'm working in a 2- to 3-foot (61–91cm) area, I use a sponge.

I look for soft, untreated sponges. The more use a sponge gets, the softer it becomes. Make sure to keep your sponge damp. When it has too much paint in it, rinse it out.

OTHER PRODUCTS

I use Vinyl Cote Flat to thin out other mediums such as Artist's Choice paints or any ready-made water-base glaze. Vinyl Cote is a water-based clear acrylic coating and comes in flat to gloss finishes. When I have done a finish with different grades of paint, the finish can look uneven. I simply roll, brush or spray Vinyl Cote over my finish to give it an even appeal. This product also comes with UV protection.

Rolco Aquasize Water-Base Gold Size is used for leafing projects. I use this sizing because it has an open time of up to thirty-six hours. It can also be used for crackling.

Krylon Webbing Spray has many uses. I like to use it to add texture to leafed walls. I've also used it for marbling.

OTHER TOOLS & SUPPLIES

Here's a listing of the tools and supplies I carry with me to a job.

- blow dryer
- brushes for oil- and water-based paints
- buckets
- craft knives
- denatured alcohol
- drop cloths
- fine steel wool
- foam brushes
- glaze (as needed for the job)
- joint compound
- ladder
- lights
- mineral spirits (odorless)
- paint (as needed for the job)
- painter's tape
- plaster blades (various sizes)
- rags
- safety razor blades
- scaffold (depending on the job)
- scissors
- screw driver with changeable tips
- sea sponges
- stain pads
- waxes
- wet-and-dry shop vac
- wire brush (for cleaning brushes)

Plaster Finishes

The first time I saw a Venetian plaster wall, I was walking through a hotel in Venice, Italy. I was told that this plaster finish was developed because of their damp, humid climate. Because Venetian plaster has a wax top coating, which creates an impenetrable finish, it is perfect for damp climates.

I thought about what I'd seen in Italy and realized that I'd found something really unique. Upon investigation, I found out that I could purchase materials in the United States, but only as white, untinted plaster. And only specific vendors could purchase it.

I learned how to use tints with the white Venetian plaster to create beautiful colors. The colored Venetian plaster can be made by anyone. I have universal tints added to the plaster to create colored Venetian plaster. Now there are even more variations in plaster. You can also purchase kits with everything you need to finish your walls. All the different plasters are interchangeable with each other, or you can have plasters custom colored from a paint store. You just need to bring in a paint color chip and have the store blend the paint with the plaster.

Some plasters are finished off with furniture wax to create a shiny, burnished look. Other plasters can be finished with a glaze to give the wall a waxed look with a sheen. Is one plaster better than another? I use all different kinds to invent my own look.

Photo courtesy of Anne Soulé, Everett & Soulé

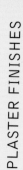

Bella Donna

JOB DESCRIPTION: Butter-gold Venetian plaster wall; Tuscan effect
SUPPLIES: 6-inch (15cm) Venetian plaster blade and a clean rag

Bella Donna was created because a client wanted a buttery yellow-gold wall color. I chose a light gold and a slightly darker gold (which you can also find on a paint chip). The client had never seen the type of wall finish I created. Because she was so thrilled with the outcome, I named this treatment after her. The client's name is Donna Dewberry and the wall finish is called "Bella Donna"—which means "beautiful woman." I think it is important that all faux finish artists who come up with a new idea should name it. By giving the wall finish a name, you are presenting an original design to the client.

light gold Venetian plaster

dark gold Venetian plaster

Walnut Liberon
Black Bison wax

Home of Marc & Donna Dewberry

The surface to be plastered should be smooth and clean. It is also a good idea for the surface to be basecoated with a color that is close to the darkest color of plaster that is going on the wall. Flat paint is the best for this procedure. Plaster does not work well on a wall that has a glossy finish.

1. SKIM ON FIRST COAT

Skim on a coat of dark gold Venetian plaster, using the 6-inch (15cm) Venetian plaster blade. Always use a thin coat. Allow plaster to dry (this takes about fifteen minutes).

2. SKIM ON SECOND COAT

Clean off your plaster blade. Randomly skim on a thin coat of the lighter gold plaster over the original darker gold plaster. Let dry.

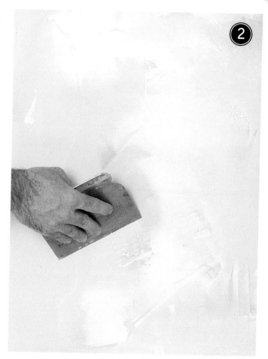

3. APPLY WAX

Skim a thin coat of Walnut wax over the entire surface.

④

PATRICK'S TIP

When applying the wax, you may notice it starting to pull up and leave a dark residue on the wall surface. If this happens, scrape off the blade and get new wax. The fresh wax will penetrate all layers. If the residue remains on the surface, leaving a dark area and scars, you can remove these areas by buffing with fine steel wool.

4. BUFF THE WAX

Buff the wax into the surface with the clean rag until you achieve a nice sheen.

BELLA DONNA FINISH

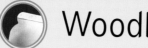

Woodbridge Red

JOB DESCRIPTION: Rich red Venetian plaster wall; aged Tuscan effect
SUPPLIES: $\frac{1}{2}$-inch (13mm) angle brush, 6-inch (15cm) Venetian plaster blade and terry cloth rag

Woodbridge Red was named after Todd Woodbridge, the Wimbledon doubles champion tennis player. I created this finish for his dining room. Because red was such a popular color at the time, this is the shade we chose.

red tinted Venetian plaster

black flat latex paint

Victorian Mahogany Liberon Black Bison wax

Home of Kara Dewberry

PATRICK'S TIP

Red is a very difficult color to apply over light or white walls. Therefore, tape off all areas and first apply a flat black paint to the surface that is going to be plastered.

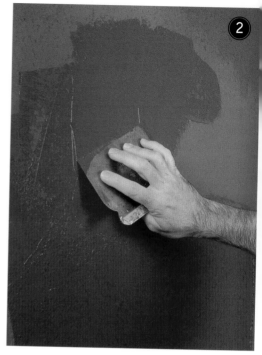

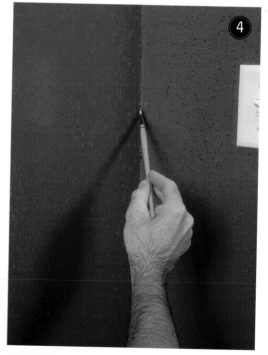

1. GETTING STARTED

Basecoat your wall with the black flat latex paint. Let dry thoroughly. Have the Venetian plaster tinted in the shade you desire. Load the blade with the Venetian plaster mix. Apply one thin coat.

2. HOW TO APPLY PLASTER

Move your whole arm—not just your wrist—as you apply the material. Never spread plaster in just one direction; apply in many different directions.

3. APPLY A SECOND COAT

Let the first coat of plaster set up and dry (plaster dries in approximately fifteen minutes, depending on weather conditions.) Apply a second, very thin coat for complete coverage.

4. TIGHT SPACES

Use your ½-inch (13mm) angle brush to apply plaster in corners and tight places. Make sure to cover all of the black basecoat color.

5. APPLY WAX
Stir the Mahogany wax thoroughly before application. Apply one thin coat of the wax with the same blade and in the same manner as the Venetian plaster.

6. BUFF THE WAX
Buff the wax into the wall in a circular motion, using a terry cloth rag.

7. CONTINUE BUFFING
Continue buffing until you achieve the sheen you desire.

WOODBRIDGE RED FINISH

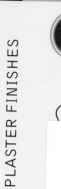

Double Fudge

JOB DESCRIPTION: Warm, chocolate-colored Venetian plaster finish with a touch of iridescent shimmer

SUPPLIES: 6-inch (15cm) Venetian plaster blade, terry cloth pad and bronze iridescent mica powder

This technique was done in a kitchen area, so I wanted a name that had a food connection. I saw chocolate brownies and came up with the name for this finish.

chocolate-fudge color Venetian plaster

Walnut Liberon Black Bison wax

Home of Amanda Dewberry

PATRICK'S TIP

When applying Venetian plaster, never move your arm in the same direction all the time. Otherwise, when you apply wax, you will see blade lines.

1. GETTING STARTED

If the texture of the wall is irregular, skim coat the wall with drywall mud prior to applying Venetian plaster. Apply two to three skim coats of the plaster. Make sure the plaster is dry before applying the next coat.

2. APPLY THE WAX & POWDER

Mix together ½-gallon (2l) Walnut wax and 4½-ounces (133ml) of the bronze iridescent powder. You can always add more bronze powder for more iridescence. Trowel onto the wall over the dry Venetian plaster.

3. BUFF THE WAX

Rub and buff off the wax with the terry cloth pad till you achieve the proper sheen.

DOUBLE FUDGE FINISH

Double Fudge Venetian plaster in the center of this ceiling decoration, home of Ray & Jan Coudriet.

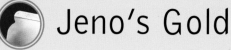

Jeno's Gold

JOB DESCRIPTION: Two-tone light and dark gold Venetian plaster finish; aged Tuscan look

SUPPLIES: 6-inch (15cm) Venetian plaster blade and terry cloth pad

This wall finish was named after my friend Lori Paulucci's son, Jeno. I told Lori that I liked to name my wall finishes after people I know. I chose to name this after Jeno because he is also artistic.

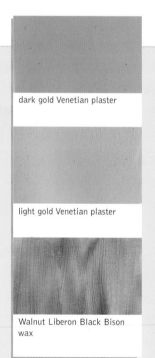

dark gold Venetian plaster

light gold Venetian plaster

Walnut Liberon Black Bison wax

Home of Amanda Dewberry

PATRICK'S TIP

Always start at the top of the wall or any other surface. That way, if you happen to drip, it is not on an area that was just completed. Apply the first coat to all walls before starting on the second coat. Do the whole room, then go back to the starting point (which should be dry now) and begin to apply a second coat.

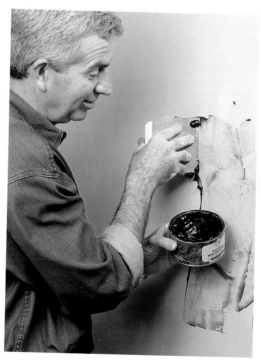

1. APPLY THE DARK GOLD PLASTER

Apply two coats of the dark gold Venetian plaster, skimmed solidly over the wall. Remember to skim it on in different directions. It takes about fifteen minutes for the Venetian plaster to set up. Let dry before applying a second coat.

2. APPLY THE LIGHT GOLD PLASTER

Apply the light gold Venetian plaster randomly, leaving spaces where the base plaster color (the dark gold) shows through.

3. APPLY THE WAX

Apply the Walnut wax in a thin skim coat completely over the surface.

Patrick Daly demonstrates how to apply wax directly from the wax container.

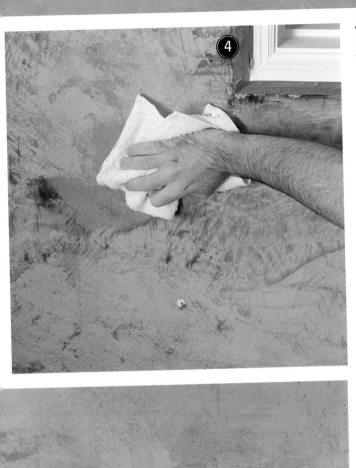

4. BUFF THE WAX
Buff and rub the wax into the surface till you achieve the desired sheen.

JENO'S GOLD FINISH

PATRICK'S TIP

Warming the can of wax in a bucket of warm water will make mixing easier.

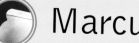 # Marcus Aurelius

JOB DESCRIPTION: Subtle light and dark gold Venetian plaster stripes
SUPPLIES: 6-inch (15cm) Venetian plaster blade, painter's tape and terry cloth pad

I chose to do this finish for a client because I needed a way to coordinate the tile color with other elements in a bathroom. This bathroom needed to complement the wall finish of the room just outside it, which was done in Jeno's Gold. So I combined a stripe of Jeno's Gold (see page 26) and a stripe of Bella Donna (see page 14) to come up with this finish.

dark gold Venetian plaster

light gold Venetian plaster

untinted white Venetian plaster

Walnut Liberon Black Bison wax

Home of Ray & Jan Coudriet

1. SKIM BELLA DONNA PLASTER

Skim light gold Venetian plaster all over your surface. Apply one full coat. Let dry.

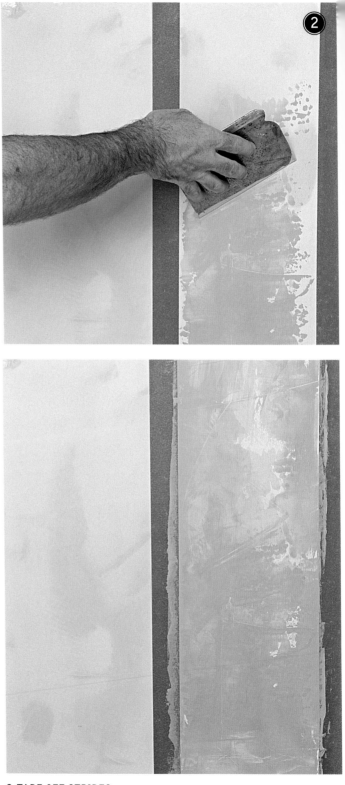

2. TAPE OFF STRIPES

Tape off the stripes, starting in the corner of the room. Tape at approximately 6-inch (15cm) intervals. Skim dark gold Venetian plaster on every other stripe.

3. SKIM ON WHITE PLASTER
Lightly skim untinted white Venetian plaster all over the room. Let dry.

4. SKIM ON WAX
Skim on Walnut wax over the entire surface.

5. BUFF THE WAX
Buff and rub the wax into the surface until you achieve the sheen you desire.

MARCUS AURELIUS FINISH

PLASTER FINISHES

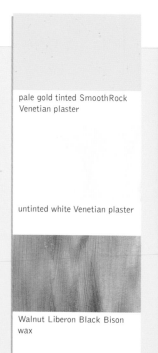

Tuscan Dream

JOB DESCRIPTION: Neutral Venetian plaster wall; heavy textured Tuscan effect
SUPPLIES: 6-inch (15cm) Venetian plaster blade and terry cloth rag

Tuscan Dream was created to cover a wall that had a heavy, textured surface. I invested in the heavy SmoothRock plaster to save time and money and take away the "orange peel" look that was originally on the walls.

This wall finish really reminded me of the walls that I'd seen on a trip to Tuscany.

pale gold tinted SmoothRock Venetian plaster

untinted white Venetian plaster

Walnut Liberon Black Bison wax

Home of Kara Dewberry

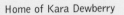

PATRICK'S TIP

If you have to leave the room during plastering, make sure to check the soles of your shoes. Plaster can be removed from carpet by water and a shop vac, if caught immediately.

1. APPLY PALE GOLD PLASTER

Trowel on pale gold Venetian plaster over the wall in a thin layer for full coverage.

2. APPLY WHITE PLASTER

Take white untinted Venetian plaster and skim over the pale gold Venetian plaster in random areas.

3. CRACKLING

If you happen to apply the plaster in a thick coat, you can use your blow dryer to create crackling. Just aim the blow dryer at the wall coated with the plaster, and you'll have a crackled effect. Do this in random areas.

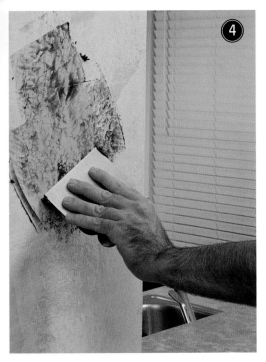

4. APPLY WAX
Load the plaster blade with Walnut wax and apply a thin coat for complete coverage.

5. REMOVE EXCESS WAX
Buff the wall and remove the excess wax with a terry cloth rag.

TUSCAN DREAM FINISH

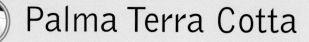

Palma Terra Cotta

JOB DESCRIPTION: Terra cotta Venetian plaster enhanced with a stenciled design

SUPPLIES: 6-inch (15cm) Venetian plaster blade, 2-inch (51mm) paint brush, stencil of your choice, painter's tape and terry cloth pad

This finish was named after a client, Mrs. Palma, who loved the color of terra cotta tiles. After experimenting for a few days, I came up with the colors she loved. So I named this wall finish after her.

dark terra cotta Venetian plaster

light terra cotta Venetian plaster

light gold Venetian plaster

Walnut Liberon Black Bison wax

PATRICK'S TIP

Do not "try" to apply complete coverage or "try" to miss spots. Just let the blade and plaster dictate where the voids will be—you do want some voids. If you "try" to miss spots, you will unconsciously make noticeable patterns in the plaster.

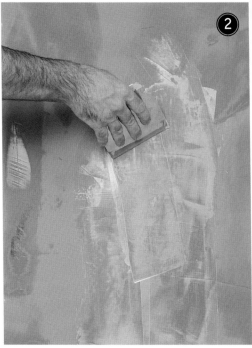

1. GETTING STARTED

Before you start applying plaster, paint the wall a color that is close to the color of the Venetian plaster. Skim coat a dark terra cotta Venetian plaster on the walls for full coverage. Always put on two coats.

2. APPLY ANOTHER PLASTER COLOR

Spread the light gold Venetian plaster sporadically and thinly over the terra cotta. Make sure you can see the terra cotta underneath.

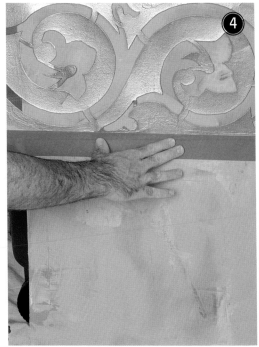

3. APPLY LIGHT TERRA COTTA PLASTER

Now apply a thin coat of a light terra cotta Venetian plaster randomly over the surface.

4. APPLY THE STENCIL

Tape the stencil to the wall.

5. CREATE A RAISED SURFACE
Take the dark terra cotta plaster and skim the plaster over the stencil. After the plaster sets up a bit, carefully pull off the stencil.

6. APPLY THE WAX
Cover your entire surface with Walnut wax. Apply the wax over the stenciled area with a brush, so you won't scrape off the stenciled plaster.

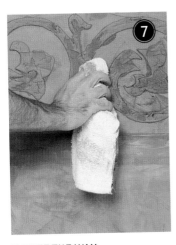

7. BUFF THE WAX
Buff the wax with a terry cloth pad.

PALMA TERRA COTTA FINISH

Faux Terrazzo Column

JOB DESCRIPTION: Faux terrazzo tile look using Venetian plaster
SUPPLIES: 6-inch (15cm) Venetian plaster blade, terry cloth pad and precast concrete column (indoor use only)

When entering a client's beautiful home, I noticed that the columns were just precast concrete. I wanted to create the look of beautiful, elegant marble columns, which would better suit the look and feel of the home. My client tells me that people come up to look at and feel the columns all the time, and are amazed that they are not real marble.

Remember, this is just one of many color combinations that can be done.

light gold Venetian plaster

dark gold Venetian plaster

chocolate-fudge color Venetian plaster

Walnut Liberon Black Bison wax

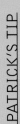

Apply wax in the same manner as you apply plaster. Don't apply the wax and then go answer the phone. If you do not buff the wax immediately after applying it, then the wax will dry and leave a noticeable dark area. You need to work the wax by applying it and then taking a rag and buffing it out before you move on to the next area.

1. APPLY PLASTER

Clean the surface using a rag and water. Skim a coat of light gold Venetian plaster; fill in any holes. Let dry. Skim on a thin layer of dark gold plaster. Make sure you have full coverage over the surface. Let dry.

2. APPLY MORE PLASTER

Skim some of the light gold Venetian plaster randomly over the surface. DO NOT let dry completely.

3. APPLY CHOCOLATE-FUDGE PLASTER

Skim on chocolate-fudge colored Venetian plaster completely over the surface.

4. WET BLENDING

Do a wet blending. Take the blade and apply a light pressure to remove some of the chocolate-fudge plaster. Clean excess plaster off your blade occasionally. Let dry completely.

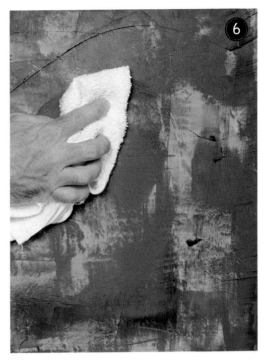

5. APPLY WAX
Cover completely with Walnut wax.

6. BUFF THE WAX
Take a terry cloth pad and buff, using a circular motion and minimal pressure to get your surface to shine.

FAUX TERRAZZO COLUMN

Snazzy Naz

JOB DESCRIPTION: Khaki Venetian plaster walls with distressed metallic stencil accents

SUPPLIES: 6-inch (15cm) Venetian plaster blade, 3-inch (8cm) foam roller, terry cloth rag, paint tray, fleur-de-lis stencil

I named this textured finish "Snazzy Naz," after my friend, architect Mark Nasrallah.

As a professional artist specializing in faux finishes, I design paint effects that fit a client's particular décor. This specialized plaster and paint technique adds elegance to the formal dining room without overwhelming the subtle beauty of the space.

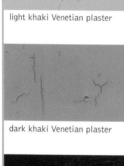

light khaki Venetian plaster

dark khaki Venetian plaster

bronze latex paint

Stripped Pine Liberon Black Bison wax

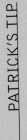

PATRICK'S TIP

It is very important to securely mask off anything that is not to receive the plaster coating. Remove all light switch covers and electrical outlet covers. Cover any furniture left in the room, the floors and any molding or walls that are not going to be plastered. Don't forget to cover the chandeliers or other light fixtures if you are doing the ceiling. And remember not to turn on those lights.

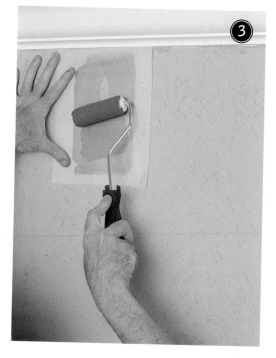

1. APPLY FIRST PLASTER COLOR

Start at the top and work your way down. Apply a thin, smooth coat of dark khaki plaster with a Venetian plaster blade. Apply the plaster in random directions. Let dry. Then apply another thin coat of plaster.

2. APPLY SECOND PLASTER COLOR

Let the dark khaki plaster dry; apply a skim coat of light khaki in the same manner as the dark khaki. If there are any dark spots, blend them into the wall with a little light khaki plaster. Let dry completely.

3. STENCIL

Measure and mark the areas for stencilling. No need to secure the stencil in place as you'll be quickly moving it around. Pour the bronze latex paint into a tray and load the foam roller. Do not saturate the roller with paint. The plastered wall has a rough texture, so apply the paint to the raised areas. This creates a soft, aged appearance. Roll the paint lightly over the stencil—you can always add more paint later if needed. Let dry.

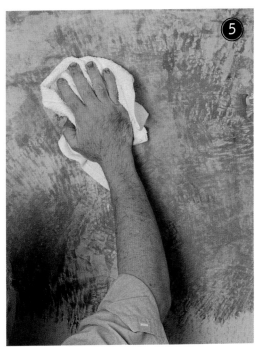

4. APPLY WAX

Work in 2–3 foot (61–91cm) sections. Use the plaster blade and apply Pine wax in the same manner as you applied the plaster. Start at the top of the wall and work your way down.

5. BUFF THE WALL

Buff the wax with a terry cloth rag before you move on to the next area. Be sure to buff the wax immediately after application, otherwise a dark spot will appear. Buff and rub until you achieve the sheen you desire.

SNAZZY NAZ FINISH

PLASTER FINISHES

Tile With Style

JOB DESCRIPTION: Faux ceramic tile
Venetian plaster wall
SUPPLIES: ½-inch (13mm) blue painter's
or grout tape, Venetian plaster blades (use
the size that best fits the size of the job),
terry cloth towel, rags, 4-inch (10cm) tile,
11" x 14" (28cm x 36cm) Bristol board
and power sander with 200-grit sandpaper

Tiled kitchen backsplashes are all
the rage, but they can be costly and
time consuming to install.
Instead, create the same
effect with paint. This faux
finishing technique has a
quick drying time and—
unlike tiling—you can easily
work around outlets and
curves without the tedium of
cutting ceramic tiles.

light khaki Venetian plaster

medium khaki Venetian plaster

dark khaki Venetian plaster

Walnut Liberon Black
Bison wax

PATRICK'S TIP

HOW TO MAKE A TEMPLATE

I used a diamond pattern, but the technique would be the same regardless of the pattern shape.

Fold a piece of Bristol board in half, across a diagonal line. Place a 4-inch (10cm) tile on the board so that one edge is even with the diagonal fold and half the tile is off the board. Trace around the tile and move it up the diagonal line, leaving a ½-inch (13mm) space between your tracing line and the edge of the tile. Trace around the tile again, continuing until you've gone off the edge of the board.

Cut out the template along the diagonal fold line and the diagonal edge of the tile that runs parallel to the fold. Don't separate the individual tiles.

1. GROUT LINES

Tape off the "grout lines" by holding the template against the wall with the bottom edge flush against the counter edge. Tape off the top diagonal edge and bottom edge of the template, leaving a "tail." The space between the two pieces of tape should be equal to the width of the 4-inch (10cm) tile template.

Move the template over so that the top edge butts up to the bottom edge of the previously taped off area. Place another piece of tape along the "new" bottom edge, continuing until all of the diagonal lines are taped. Then, turn the template over so it "leans" in the other direction and place crossing pieces of tape to create the diamond shapes.

2. APPLY DARK KHAKI PLASTER

Using a Venetian plaster blade, randomly apply a smooth coat of the dark khaki plaster. Work top to bottom. Complete an entire section, then move to the next section. Let dry. Add a second coat and let dry.

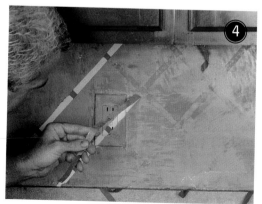

3. APPLY MEDIUM KHAKI PLASTER

Apply a thin layer of the medium khaki shade of plaster. Let dry completely.

4. REMOVE THE TAPE

Carefully remove the tape, starting with the last piece applied. It's okay if a little plaster chips around the edges; it adds to the natural appearance. If large pieces chip, apply new plaster layers, starting with the darkest color. Let dry.

5. APPLY LIGHT KHAKI PLASTER
Apply a thin layer of the light khaki plaster to the entire area with the plaster blade, even over the "grout" lines. Let dry.

6. SAND OVER THE TILES
Once dry, use the power sander and lightly sand over random tiles to vary their color. Remove the dust with a wet cloth.

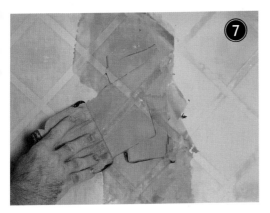

7. APPLY WAX
Apply the Walnut wax using the plaster blade, working in 2–3 foot (61–91cm) sections. Start at the top and work your way down, applying the wax in the same manner as the plaster.

8. BUFF THE WAX
Buff immediately with a terry cloth rag or towel. Continue working in small sections until you've covered the entire surface.

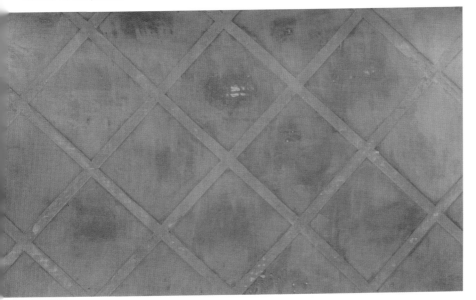

TILE WITH
STYLE
FINISH

Kitchen Cabinet Finishes

I've discovered that when people are going to buy or sell a home, they find that their kitchen needs some updating. They want to replace their cabinets and countertops. First, they go to the cabinet shop. Next, I'll get a phone call. I'll meet my client, we look at the cabinets they like and then they ask me to replicate the finish on their cabinets.

After basecoating the doors and the rest of the cabinet, I take an oil-based glaze and apply it with a brush. I move it around the cabinet, wipe off the excess and then quickly apply a lacquer or shellac to keep the finish from "moving." Next day I'll finish the cabinet with a satin or gloss varnish to protect it.

Home of Ray & Jan Coudriet

Cookies & Cream

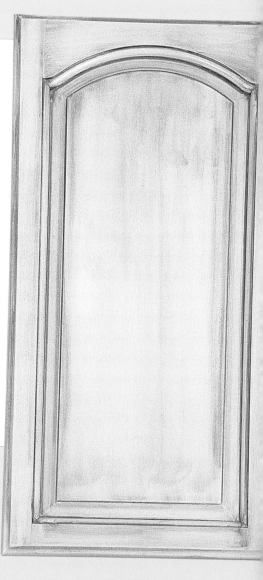

JOB DESCRIPTION: Soft, neutral painted cabinet finish

SUPPLIES: paint brush (size appropriate for this project), cotton rag, lacquer thinner, clear spray shellac and satin or gloss varnish

I walked into a house that had countertops replaced with granite and new tile on the floor. I had already decided to put Venetian plaster on the walls and I wanted something softer on the cabinets, so that the countertops and walls would stand out. Cookies & Cream was a finish that wouldn't compete with these elements.

cream color Breakthrough satin paint

Raw Umber Nu-Glaze

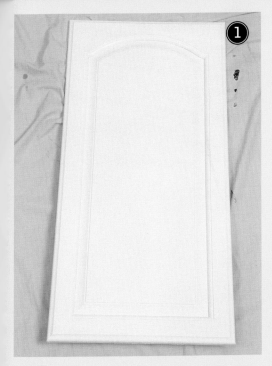

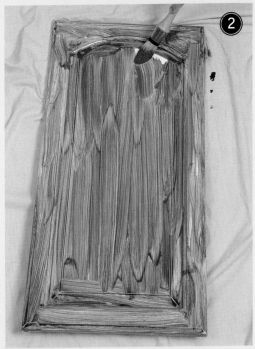

1. BASECOAT

Wipe down the door with lacquer thinner to clean off the old finish. Paint the door with a cream colored Breakthrough satin.

2. APPLY GLAZE

Take Raw Umber Nu-Glaze and brush it all over the door. Paint quickly because the glaze will seep through.

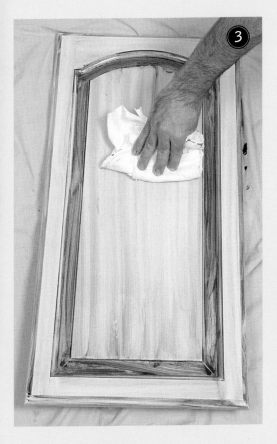

3. CREATING THE FINISH

Take a rag and wipe off in the direction of the panels—wipe down one side, across the bottom, up the other side and across the top. Wipe the beveled part of the cabinet last. Make sure to wipe off in one straight stroke—don't stop halfway on the cabinet. Spray with clear shellac to protect the glaze and to keep the glaze from "moving." When dry, paint on satin or gloss varnish.

Large Crackle

JOB DESCRIPTION: Rustic crackle cabinet finish

SUPPLIES: chip brush, 2-inch (51mm) fitch brush, 6-inch (15cm) roller, round mop brush, soft, cotton rag and crackling medium

This is better as a small project, because the crackle isn't going to be consistent on every cabinet. The finish gives a room a rustic look. You can also do this on chairs, small tables and shutters.

taupe color Breakthrough satin paint

cream color Breakthrough satin paint

Jacobean Minwax gel stain

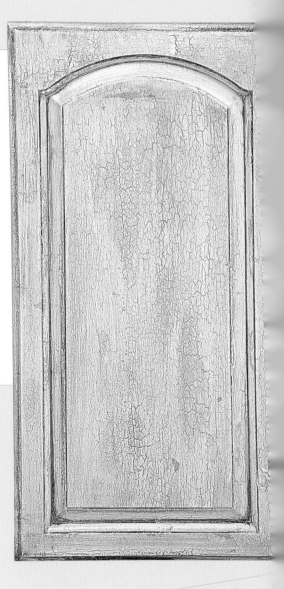

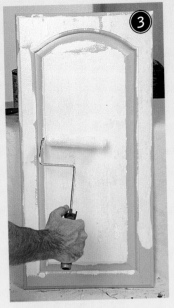

1. BASECOAT
Basecoat the cabinet with taupe paint. Make sure to use two coats for full coverage.

2. APPLY CRACKLING MEDIUM
Apply crackling medium with a fitch brush and let dry completely.

3. APPLY CREAM PAINT
Apply cream paint with a 6-inch (15cm) roller over the crackling medium. Use a small brush to paint in the crevices. Then let dry thoroughly.

4. APPLY STAIN
Mop on Jacobean stain all over the surface using a mop brush.

5. FINISHING
Rub off the stain with a soft, cotton cloth. Notice the crackles in the finish!

Porcelain Crackle

JOB DESCRIPTION: Fine, faint crackle cabinet finish
SUPPLIES: small paintbrush, 6-inch (15cm) roller and crackling medium

This finish gives your cabinets an antique look. It creates a very faint crackle. Again, you'd probably want to do this as a small project, because the crackle will not be consistent on every cabinet. This is also a great finish for a table top, lamp, mantel and armoire.

white
Breakthrough paint

yellow-cream
Breakthrough paint

1. BASECOAT
Basecoat with white Breakthrough paint.

2. APPLY CRACKLING MEDIUM
Apply crackling medium all over the cabinet with a brush. Let dry thoroughly—till there is a sheen and is not sticky to the touch.

3. APPLY SECOND PAINT COLOR
With a 6-inch (15cm) roller, apply a coat of yellow-cream paint. Roll the area with a consistent speed. Let dry and the crackle will appear.

Antique Celadon

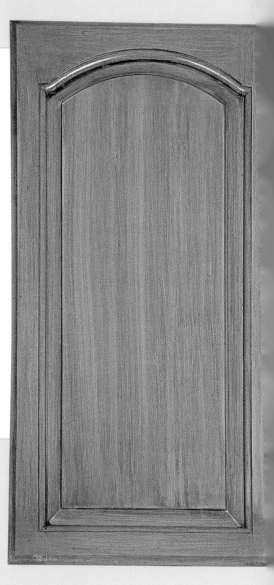

JOB DESCRIPTION: Cabinetry with an antique celadon finish
SUPPLIES: chip brush, flogger brush, soft cotton rag, lacquer thinner, spray shellac and satin or gloss varnish

"What's old is new again!" I found that everyone loved this green. I came up with this finish for kitchen island cabinets (making them different from the other cabinets), and tables and chair legs. This is a great finish not only for cabinetry but also for headboards and children's bedroom furniture, because painted furniture is so popular.

celadon green color
Breakthrough satin paint

Burnt Umber Nu-Glaze

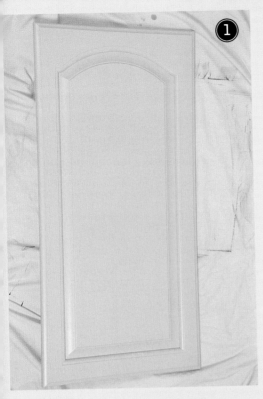

1. BASECOAT

Clean the cabinet with lacquer thinner. Paint the cabinet with a celadon green satin paint.

2. APPLY GLAZE

Apply Burnt Umber Nu-Glaze all over the cabinet. Apply glaze in the direction of the panels—down one side, across the bottom, up the other side and across the top. Apply to the beveled area last.

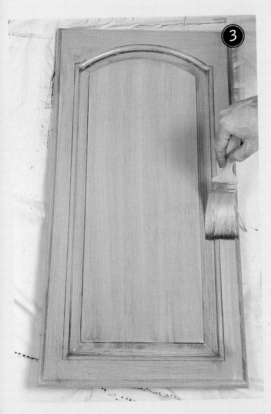

3. FINISHING STEP

Wipe off the glaze with a soft, cotton cloth. Make sure to follow through in one stroke—don't stop halfway. Wipe off the beveled area last. Then follow up with a flogger brush, using it to soften the glaze finish. Spray with shellac to keep the glaze from "moving." Allow to dry thoroughly. Paint on several coats of satin or gloss varnish to protect the finish.

Faux Mahogany

JOB DESCRIPTION: Rich, mahogany-look cabinet finish

SUPPLIES: paint brush (size appropriate for this project), flogger brush, lacquer thinner, spray shellac and satin or gloss varnish

I've used this finish on cabinetry that has been painted a few times. When the client replaced their countertops and appliances, they wanted a rich-looking wood cabinet. That's why I created Faux Mahogany. This is also perfect for metal doors, giving them a rich wood-look finish.

light gold color Breakthrough satin paint

Burnt Umber Nu-Glaze

Van Dyke Brown Nu-Glaze

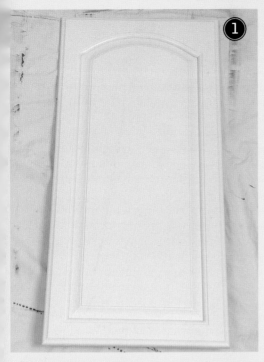

1. BASECOAT

Clean the cabinet first with lacquer thinner. Basecoat with a light gold color Breakthrough satin. Let dry.

2. APPLY FIRST GLAZE

Use a size-appropriate paint brush to apply Burnt Umber Nu-Glaze randomly over the cabinet.

3. APPLY SECOND GLAZE

Take Van Dyke Brown Nu-Glaze and paint randomly over the cabinet.

4. FINISHING STEP

Blend the stains together with a flogger brush. Spray with shellac to keep the glaze from "moving." Let dry, then paint on several coats of satin or gloss varnish.

KITCHEN CABINET FINISHES

Barnyard Red

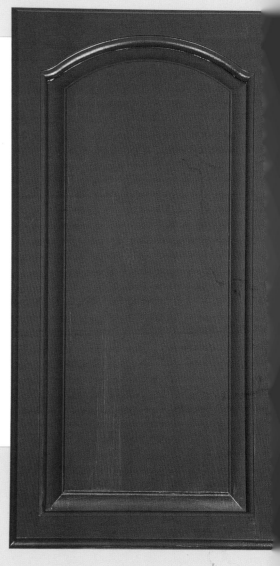

JOB DESCRIPTION: Red cabinet with a glazed topcoat
SUPPLIES: chip brush, lacquer thinner, clear spray shellac, satin or gloss varnish and soft, cotton rag

I've used this application many times on chairs, lamp bases, desks and pieces of furniture that "make a statement," as well as on cabinetry. The kitchens with this look frequently have a French country theme. It's great with brick floors and modern country accessories. Usually I'll paint the kitchen chairs to coordinate with the cabinets.

cedar color Breakthrough satin paint

Raw Umber Nu-Glaze

1. BASECOAT
Clean the cabinet with lacquer thinner. Paint with cedar color Breakthrough satin paint.

2. APPLY GLAZE
Take the Raw Umber Nu-Glaze and paint all over the cabinet. Make sure to paint in the same direction on each of the panels—down one side, across the bottom, up the other side and across the top. Make sure not to stop halfway through a stroke.

3. WIPE OFF THE GLAZE
Wipe off the glaze lightly with a soft, cotton rag, again following the direction of the wood. Apply clear shellac to protect the glaze and keep it from "moving." Let dry. Paint on several coats of satin or gloss varnish.

Candy Licorice

JOB DESCRIPTION: Oriental-look cabinetry

SUPPLIES: no. 4 round brush, 3-inch (8cm) foam roller, lacquer thinner, clear spray shellac, satin or gloss varnish

I use this cabinet finish frequently in powder rooms and on bedroom end tables. It creates a high-end Oriental look. Take your time when applying the black paint so that you'll have just the right amount of red paint showing underneath. Adding gold hand painting or gilding makes it to "die faux."

red color Breakthrough satin paint

black Breakthrough satin paint

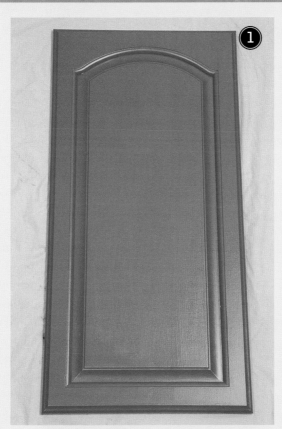

1. BASECOAT

Take lacquer thinner and wipe down the cabinet door well. Use a 3-inch (8cm) foam roller and basecoat the cabinet with red Breakthrough paint. When dry, repaint the cabinet door using a brush and the same color. Let cure and harden for twenty-four hours.

2. APPLY BLACK PAINT

Stroke black Breakthrough paint in one direction, randomly over the cabinet. Dip the brush into a bit of water to loosen up the brush and to slightly thin the paint. Let dry thoroughly.

Spray with clear shellac to protect and keep the color from "moving." Let dry. Paint several coats of satin or gloss varnish to protect the finish.

Shabby Yet Chic

JOB DESCRIPTION: Light, rustic cabinet
SUPPLIES: no. 6 round brush, 2-inch
(51mm) fitch brush and damp rag

This look has been done for years in
beach houses or in homes with a
rustic look. It works well with pine
or light floors. It's a charming and
light look—a less-is-more look.

light gold color Breakthrough
satin paint

white acrylic paint

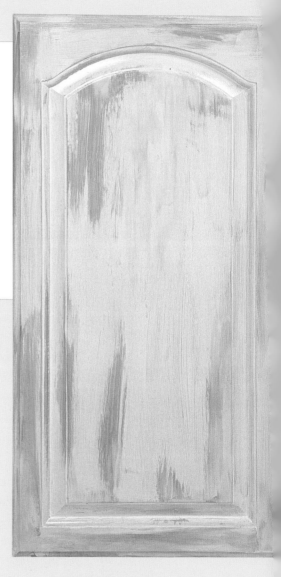

1. BASECOAT
Basecoat the cabinet door with light gold color Breakthrough paint, using the no. 6 round brush. Let dry.

2. ADD WHITE PAINT
Paint over the light gold color on the cabinet with white acrylic paint. Use a 2-inch (51mm) fitch brush to fill in the crevices.

3. CREATE THE "SHABBY" LOOK
With a damp rag, randomly rub off some of the top layer of paint. Then make sure to seal the finish.

More Fantastic Finishes

Featured in this chapter are finishes that can be used on furniture, ceilings, wall molding, metal and walls.

You'll find techniques that show you how to create faux wood grain and leather finishes and how to use silver and gold leaf to imitate antique gilding. There's also instruction in this chapter for a faux stone walkway and a faux wood door. Plus other quick and easy wall finishes are included in this section.

Use your imagination to find ways to embellish your home.

Photo Courtesy of Anne Soulé, Everett & Soulé

Rub & Run

JOB DESCRIPTION: Antique, aged wall
SUPPLIES: 2-inch (51mm) fitch brush, terry cloth pad and squeeze bottle

My Rub & Run finish is created using Porter Paint PORTERDECK Semi-Transparent Stain. You can choose from several different stain colors—pick the color that works best with your décor. Apply it over any eggshell or satin paint.

I accidentally came up with this finish. I was frustrated on a job and threw a cloth pad covered with stain on the wall. Someone told me the client was headed my way, so I started wiping the stain off the wall. He walked up to me and told me how much he loved what I was doing on the wall! Thus Rub & Run was born.

Rub & Run paint/glaze formula

Home of Ray & Jan Coudriet

GETTING STARTED
Prep your wall by painting with an eggshell or satin finish. This wall has been basecoated with an antique white.

1. EASY APPLICATION
Pour the stain into a squeeze bottle. Squirt some stain onto a terry cloth pad.

2. APPLY TO WALL
Rub onto the wall in a circular motion. Work in 2–3 foot (61–91cm) sections.

3. SOFTEN THE FINISH
After you have applied stain to a wall section, immediately take a fitch brush and brush over the finish to soften and remove any swirls created by the terry cloth pad.

RUB & RUN FINISH

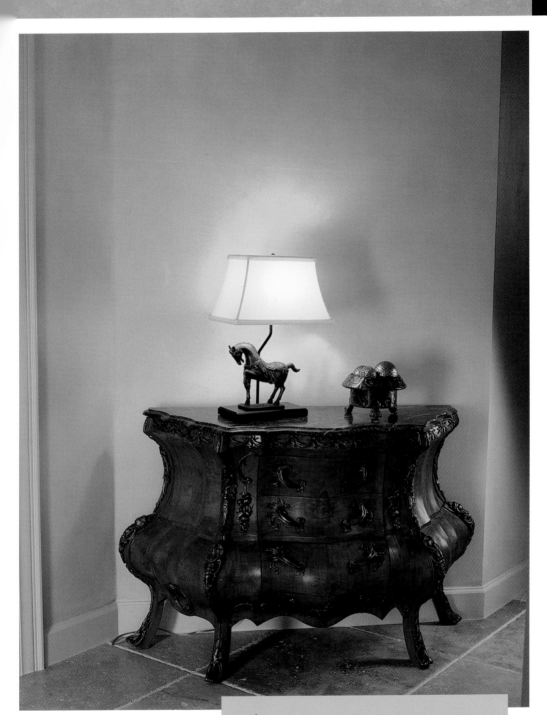

Home of Ray & Jan Coudriet

PATRICK'S TIP

Since this project contains an exterior stain, make sure you have adequate ventilation. Rub & Run uses a semi-transparent stain that does not soak into a painted surface. It stays on top of the wall and is rubbed and brushed to achieve an aged appearance.

It's Here But It's Not There

JOB DESCRIPTION: Very subtle wall stenciling treatment
SUPPLIES: 3-inch (8cm) foam roller, masking tape, Plaid stencil #26777 Damask Tapestry

I came up with this wall finish because I had a client who said that she wanted a faux finish on her wall but she "didn't want to see it." On further questioning, she told me she wanted more than just a flat finish, she wanted some "movement." Through some trial and error, I developed this technique. It's very subtle, yet sophisticated and very easy to live with. Don't limit yourself to the green colors shown.

celery green latex paint

celery green latex paint
(custom mixed to be slightly lighter than wall color)

Home of Amanda Dewberry

PATRICK'S TIP

Make sure your "shadow" paint color contrasts enough with the wall color.

GETTING STARTED
Basecoat your wall in the slightly darker wall color.

1. PAINT THE WALLS, STENCIL

Paint your walls with the slightly darker color. Tape your stencil on the wall and roll the slightly lighter color on the stencil, working down the wall. Space the stenciled stripes around the room and mark the walls. Let paint dry thoroughly before proceeding to step 2.

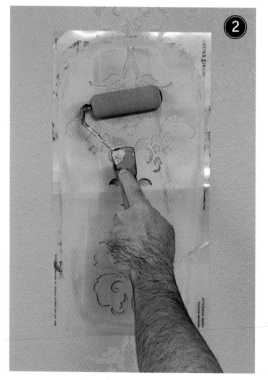

2. CREATE A SHADOW

Move the stencil just slightly lower from where it was placed before and tape it to the wall. Roll on the same lighter paint color to create a shadow effect.

IT'S HERE BUT IT'S NOT THERE FINISH

Easy Striping

JOB DESCRIPTION: Casual, striped walls
SUPPLIES: 6-inch (15cm) roller and 2-inch (51mm) China bristle brush

This is an easy technique. You don't want it to look too "finished," so there's no need to tape off walls or do a lot of measuring. I came up with this paint technique because I am often asked to do something in laundry rooms, something that is fairly fast and easy. I coordinate the colors to the walls outside the room I'm striping, so you can use any color combination.

Antique White
Sherwin-Williams satin paint

Wild Bamboo
Sherwin-Williams satin paint

Home of Ray & Jan Coudriet

PATRICK'S TIP

When painting any kind of a wall striping technique, always start your first stripe in the most inconspicuous corner of the room to leave some room for error. For this technique, don't measure—just paint!

GETTING STARTED
Basecoat the walls with Wild Bamboo. Make sure the walls are completely covered. Let walls dry thoroughly.

1. PAINT FIRST STRIPE
Use the 6-inch (15cm) roller, with Antique White, and roll one stripe (the width of the roller), starting in the corner.

2. SECOND STRIPE
Measure the width of the roller for the second stripe (which is actually the base color, Wild Bamboo). Do not paint—this is just to measure for your next stripe.

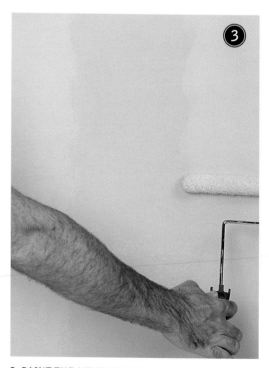

3. PAINT THE NEXT STRIPES
Paint the next stripe just like the first stripe, using the 6-inch (15cm) roller and Antique White. For the next stripe, follow step 2. Then alternate with step 1, etc.

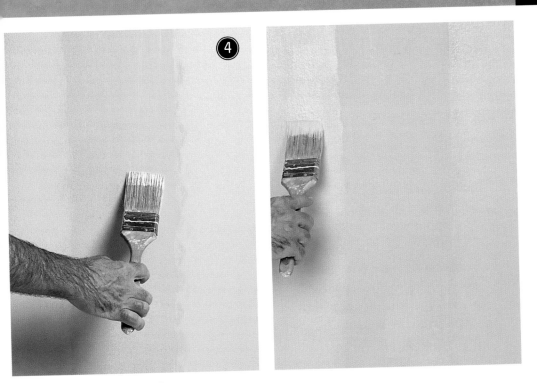

4. DRYBRUSH ON THE STRIPES

Take a 2-inch (51mm) China bristle brush and place a small amount of Wild Bamboo on it. Wipe off any excess paint. Drybrush the Wild Bamboo on the Antique White stripe. Then drybrush the Antique White on the Wild Bamboo stripe. Repeat around the room.

EASY STRIPING FINISH

Simple Wood Grain

JOB DESCRIPTION: Warm, wood-look finish
SUPPLIES: 2-inch (51mm) fitch brush,
4-inch (102mm) brush, softening brush,
mineral spirits, graining tool and lacquer

I came up with this through trial and
error—trying to match a metal door
to the woodwork. I've used this
technique for about ten years and it's
still popular.

Raffia Basket
Sherwin-Williams satin paint

Dark Red Mahogany Nu-Glaze

Van Dyke Brown Nu-Glaze

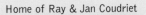

Home of Ray & Jan Coudriet

If you are working on a door that has a "cut" in it—a change of grain direction or a panel—you should tape off each section. Work one section, apply a quick-drying sealer, let it dry and then work the next area. After all sections are complete, apply another coat of the sealer.

GETTING STARTED
Paint your surface with Raffia
Basket paint. Let dry completely.

1. USE FIRST GLAZE
Use a 4-inch (102mm) paint brush
with Dark Red Mahogany Nu-
Glaze (thinned with mineral spirits) and paint long, vertical lines.

2. EXAMPLE OF GLAZE ON SURFACE
This is your pattern. Note that the Dark Red
Mahogany Nu-Glaze does not completely cover.

3. APPLY SECOND GLAZE
Use the 2-inch (51mm) fitch and Van Dyke Brown
Nu-Glaze to paint long vertical lines to fill in the
lighter areas.

4. BLEND
Blend and soften your glazes together with the 2-inch
(51mm) fitch brush.

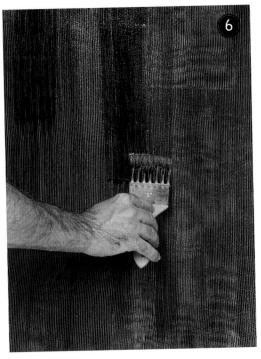

5. CREATE GRAINING

Take a graining tool and pull it down in one continuous vertical line. Do this all the way across your surface. Then soften with the softening brush, again pulling in a continuous vertical line.

6. BLEND & SOFTEN

Use the 2-inch (51mm) fitch and gently brush over your surface to blend and soften. Do this randomly, leaving a few of the wood-grain lines. Seal with lacquer immediately.

SIMPLE WOOD GRAIN FINISH

Old Man Leather

JOB DESCRIPTION: Rich, leather-look wall finish

SUPPLIES: 2-inch (51mm) fitch brush, 6-inch (15cm) roller, sea sponge, staining pad and satin polyurethane

This is a look I used a lot for an interior designer I worked with. It involves some trial and error, sponging on and sponging off, until you get the look you like. This is a very rich and classic look.

Raffia Basket
Sherwin-Williams satin paint

Raw Umber Artist's Choice
water-based glaze

Burnt Umber Artist's Choice
water-based glaze

Jacobean Minwax
penetrating stain

Home of Ray & Jan Coudriet

PATRICK'S TIP

Move quickly and keep your movements random. You will be moving in all directions, but avoid making circles.

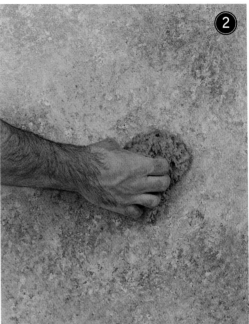

1. BASECOAT & APPLY FIRST GLAZE

Basecoat your surface with Raffia Basket. Use your 6-inch (15cm) roller and Raw Umber glaze (saturated but not dripping) and roll on in different directions.

2. USE THE SEA SPONGE

After you've rolled all over your surface, use a sea sponge and pounce over your surface (twist your sponge and wrist from right to left) to blend the sponged surface.

3. ROLL OVER THE SURFACE

Roll over again with the roller and Burnt Umber glaze. Move your roller in different directions. Then sponge and pounce over your surface with Burnt Umber (as in step 2). Let dry.

4. APPLY PENETRATING STAIN

Mix one part polyurethane and two parts Jacobean stain; then apply into a staining pad. Using a "wiggling" motion, work in small areas in a downward diagonal direction. Then move in an upward diagonal direction, similar to making a V or an X.

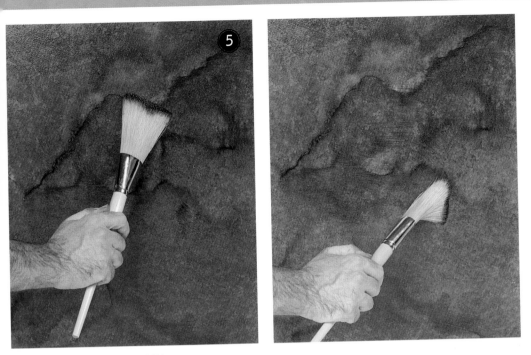

5. CREATE THE LEATHER LOOK

Use a 2-inch (51mm) fitch to soften the lines and to create veins and seams in the "leather." Avoid making the lines straight—try to curve them slightly to create natural vein and seam effects.

OLD MAN LEATHER FINISH

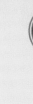

Sueded Wall

JOB DESCRIPTION: Sophisticated, rich suede wall

SUPPLIES: 2-inch (51mm) fitch brush and sea sponge

I had a client show me a finish she liked and wanted me to come up with a similar look that wasn't oil-based. I try to use water-based products whenever I can, even though they require me to work faster, since they dry more quickly.

Raffia Basket
Sherwin-Williams satin paint

Raw Umber Artist's Choice
water-based glaze

Home of Ray & Jan Coudriet

GETTING STARTED
Basecoat the wall with Raffia Basket. Let dry.

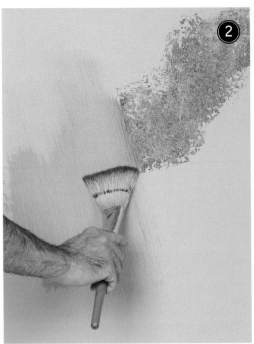

2. BRUSH OUT SPONGING
Use the 2-inch (51mm) fitch and brush out the sponged designs.

1. SPONGE ON GLAZE
Wet the sea sponge, then wring it out until it is just damp. Dip the sponge into the Raw Umber glaze, remove excess glaze and lightly pounce on the wall. Start at the top of the wall and work a small section at a time.

3. SPONGE AGAIN
Continue to pounce the glaze on another part of the wall with the sea sponge.

4. BRUSH OUT AGAIN
Again, brush out the pounced area.

5. POUNCE OVER THE AREA AGAIN
Pounce over the area you first worked on. Then brush off again. Repeat the process until you achieve the desired effect.

SUEDED WALL FINISH

Gold Leaf Iron Railing

JOB DESCRIPTION: Rich gold-leaf accents on a plain, black wrought-iron railing
SUPPLIES: small fitch brush, soft artist brush, Rolco Aquasize water-base gold size and clear spray shellac

I have a lot of clients who ask for gilding on different surfaces. I can achieve a great look with imitation gold leaf and Rolco sizing. It's an "old-world" gilded look, but for a lot less time and money.

gold leaf

Van Dyke Brown Nu-Glaze

Home of Amanda Dewberry

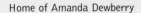

Tape off any and all areas that will not receive gold or silver leaf. One of the steps for this technique requires spraying adhesive on the surface to receive leafing. Apply adhesive to the area that will be leafed and allow the glue to set up, which usually takes about fifteen minutes.

1. APPLY THE SIZE
Apply the Rolco Aquasize water-base gold size. Tear off a strip of gold leaf and apply it to the railing handle.

2. SMOOTH THE GOLD LEAF
Smooth the gold leaf onto the railing and remove the paper backing.

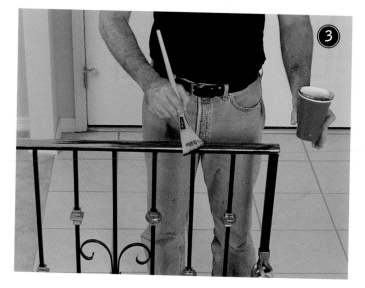

3. APPLY GLAZE
Use the small fitch brush to apply Van Dyke Brown glaze.

4. SOFTEN THE GLAZE

Use a soft artist brush to soften the glaze. Use a circular motion and gentle pressure.

5. SEAL THE GOLD LEAFING

To seal, spray with a clear shellac.

Gold Leaf Medallion

JOB DESCRIPTION: Antique-look gold-leafed ceiling medallion

SUPPLIES: chip brush, large softening brush, badger hair brush, Rolco Aquasize water-base gold size, Zinsser Bulls Eye Clear spray shellac, white polystyrene medallion and cotton rag

This is an easy way to gild a medallion, but you still get a very elegant look. These medallions can be used in a dining room or an entryway. You don't have to use it with a light fixture— buy a medallion without the hole in the center and place it on the ceiling to add a formal, classic touch.

black satin paint

gold leaf

Van Dyke Brown
Nu-Glaze

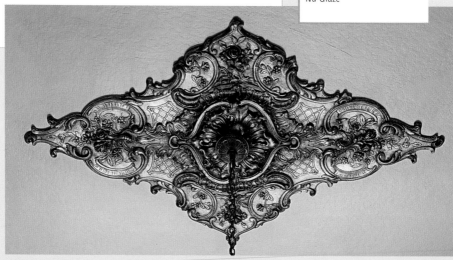

Close-up of gold leaf medallion, home of Ray & Jan Coudriet

Home of Ray & Jan Coudriet

1. BASECOAT THE MEDALLION & SIZE

Basecoat the medallion with black satin paint. Use a chip brush and apply Rolco Aquasize water-base gold size to the medallion. Let it set up for about fifteen minutes—it will become clear instead of a milky color.

2. APPLY GOLD LEAF

When the sizing is tacky, tear off random pieces of gold leaf and place on the medallion.

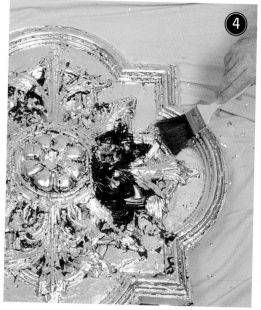

3. APPLY ADDITIONAL GOLD LEAF

Pull off the backing and press more gold leaf onto the medallion. Continue to tear off random pieces of gold leaf and place all over the medallion.

4. CONTINUE WORKING WITH THE LEAF

At this point there will be lots of leaf flakes everywhere. Use the softening brush to grab the flakes and push them into the small crevices.

5. CLEAN UP GOLD LEAF FLAKES

Use a badger hair brush and pounce the gold leaf flakes into all the small crevices. Leave no part uncovered. Then brush over the medallion to clean off the loose flakes.

6. APPLY GLAZE

Paint the Van Dyke Brown glaze over the entire surface. Use a rag made from soft, cotton t-shirt material and rub off the excess glaze. Use the softening brush and a very light circular motion to get rid of drag lines and streaks in the glaze.

7. APPLY SEALER

Spray with Zinsser Bulls Eye Clear spray shellac to finish and protect the gold-leaf finish and seal the glaze.

COMPLETED GOLD LEAF MEDALLION

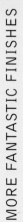

Stencil on Silver Leaf

JOB DESCRIPTION: Elegant silver-leafed wall with burnished stenciling
SUPPLIES: 2-inch (51mm) fitch brush, badger hair brush, 3-inch (8cm) foam roller, Rolco Aquasize water-base gold size, Zinsser Bulls Eye Clear spray shellac, Zinsser Bulls Eye Amber shellac, Zinsser Bulls Eye Clear shellac, stencil and cotton rag

I was asked to imitate a wallpaper, but the client wanted the finish painted directly on the wall. This gave the client the same look for a lot less money. This technique is a little more time consuming, but I think the elegant result is worth it!

silver leaf
(6-inch or 15cm roll)

Metallic Silver Artist's Choice
water-based glaze

Van Dyke Brown Nu-Glaze

cedar color Breakthrough paint

Taupe Artist's Choice
water-based glaze

Home of Ray & Jan Coudriet

1. BASECOAT & APPLY SIZE

Basecoat the walls with cedar color Breakthrough paint. Use a 3-inch (8cm) foam roller and apply the Rolco Aquasize water-base gold size. Roll over the surface completely. Let it set up for about fifteen minutes—it will become clear instead of a milky color.

2. APPLY SILVER LEAF

Cut the silver leaf in 6-inch (15cm) squares. Peel off paper backing and apply to the wall (shiny side to the sticky surface). Continue to apply silver leaf, but let some of the cedar background color show through.

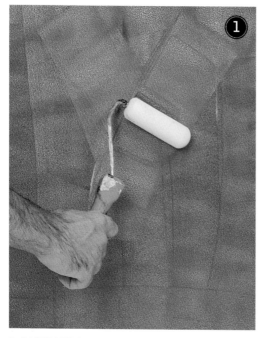

3. APPLY GLAZE

Mix two parts Metallic Silver glaze with one part Taupe glaze. Place stencil on wall surface and roll on the glaze mixture, using a 3-inch (8cm) foam roller. Continue to move the stencil and roll on the glaze.

4. APPLY BROWN GLAZE

Paint the Van Dyke Brown glaze randomly over the surface with a 2-inch (51mm) fitch brush. Pat and rub off the glaze with a cotton rag.

5. SOFTEN THE GLAZE
Lightly and randomly brush over the surface with a badger hair brush to soften the glaze.

6. PROTECT THE WALL SURFACE
Spray your surface with Bulls Eye Clear spray shellac in a well-ventilated area. Always wear protective gear.

7. APPLY COLORED GLAZE
Mix two parts Bulls Eye Amber and one part Bulls Eye Clear shellac and apply in random areas.

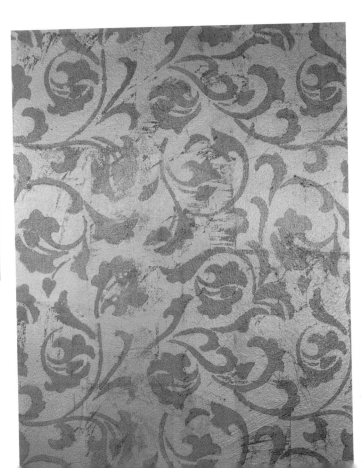

STENCIL ON SILVER LEAF FINISH

Silver Leaf Medallion

JOB DESCRIPTION: Ceiling medallion with an antiqued finish

SUPPLIES: chip brush, large softening brush, badger hair brush, Rolco Aquasize water-base gold size, Zinsser Bulls Eye Amber shellac, Zinsser Bulls Eye Clear shellac, white polystyrene medallion and cotton rag

For my clients who like the look of silver instead of gold, I came up with this technique. It gives the look of old silver (without the tarnish).

silver leaf

cedar color Breakthrough paint

Van Dyke Brown Nu-Glaze

Close-up of silver leaf medallion, home of Ray & Jan Coudriet

1. BASECOAT

Basecoat the medallion with cedar color Breakthrough paint.

Follow steps 2–7 of the Gold Leaf Medallion technique on pages 104–105, substituting silver leaf for gold leaf.

2. APPLY GLAZE

Use Van Dyke Brown glaze to age the silver leaf. Be sure to apply with a heavy hand.

3. EXCESS GLAZE

Remove excess glaze with a clean cotton rag.

4. SOFTENING BRUSH

Using a circular motion, take the softening brush and remove glaze lines on the medallion. Then seal the aged finish with Zinsser Bulls Eye Clear Shellac.

5. APPLY AMBER SHELLAC

Mix two parts Zinsser Bulls Eye Amber shellac to one part Zinsser Bulls Eye Clear shellac. Paint the shellac mixture over the entire surface.

COMPLETED SILVER LEAF MEDALLION

MORE FANTASTIC FINISHES

Walk This Way

JOB DESCRIPTION: Create a beautiful stone walkway

SUPPLIES: 2-inch (51mm) Chinese bristle brush, long, stiff-bristled brush, 1-inch (3cm) trim roller, 9-inch (23cm) roller, large sea sponge, solvent-based polyurethane, paint tray and rag

Transform a sound but unsightly walkway into a beautiful brick path with an easy faux finish. You don't even have to worry about precision, since an uneven pattern creates a much more natural effect.

This front walkway was stained and dingy from years of high traffic. However, the concrete was sound and hadn't developed any cracks. So a fresh look was created that is more inviting, appealing and, of course, artistic.

Light Gray Breakthrough paint

Rust Breakthrough paint

Dark Raw Umber Breakthrough paint

Jacobean Minwax Wood Finish stain

GETTING STARTED
Clean off the walkway, removing any loose dirt and debris. Using a paint roller, basecoat the entire walkway with Light Gray Break-through paint. Let dry completely.

2. APPLY DARK RAW UMBER PAINT
Apply Dark Raw Umber paint as you applied the Rust paint in step 1. Don't completely cover the previous paint layer.

1. APPLY RUST PAINT
Moisten a sea sponge with water till it's just slightly damp. Lightly dab Rust paint onto only one side of the sea sponge. Dab the paint onto the entire walkway with a random twisting motion. Don't make a uniform pattern or cover the surface completely. Let dry.

3. ADD "MORTAR" LINES
Cut notches out of the sides of a 1-inch (3cm) trim roller, so it creates a rough, uneven surface. Load the roller with Light Gray paint and roll mortar lines to define the stone shapes. Vary the shape and size for a more natural look.

4. BLEND THE "MORTAR" LINES

Load a long, stiff-bristled brush with a touch of Light Gray, then wipe the brush on a rag to remove excess paint. Using a light touch, softly blend along the mortar lines and add a bit of this color randomly to the stones. Don't wash this brush.

5. SOFTEN "MORTAR" LINES

Use Dark Raw Umber or Rust and the same dirty brush to soften the color along the mortar lines. Then soften the color of the stones, using a large sea sponge. Occasionally stand back to assess which areas need additional work. Let dry completely.

6. FINISHING TOUCHES

Mix one part Jacobean stain and one part solvent-based polyurethane and apply this mixture to the mortar lines using a Chinese bristle brush. Allow some areas to be darker than others to create an aged appearance. Let dry completely.

For additional protection, apply two or three coats of solvent-based polyurethane with a brush or 9-inch (23cm) roller.

Door Prize

JOB DESCRIPTION: Transforming a metal door into one with a mahogany finish

SUPPLIES: 2-inch (51mm) nylon brush for water-based paints, large mop brush, rags and 150–200 grit sandpaper

A mahogany finish adds warm, rich color to a home. I painted a faux mahogany finish on this front door to create that warmth and elegance. You can adapt this paint finish to fit any surface. The glaze is semi-transparent, so the underlying layers remain visible.

light gold Breakthrough paint

mahogany color tinted glaze

Van Dyke Brown color tinted glaze

Home of Marcus & Lynn Dewberry

PATRICK'S TIP

For a more natural appearance, leave the glaze darkest in the corners and around the outer edges of the door and panels.

1. BASECOAT

Use a 2-inch (51mm) nylon brush to basecoat the door with the Breakthrough paint. Let dry thoroughly.

2. APPLY FIRST GLAZE

Apply the first coat of mahogany glaze with even strokes, starting at the top and dragging to the bottom in one motion, using the mop brush. Then flip the brush and stroke over the same application, working from the bottom to the top, connecting the first and second strokes.

If your door has panels, start with the vertical sides and then the horizontal cross pieces, finishing with the panels.

Try to work with the "cuts" (see page 124 of the Faux Finish Terminology section)—the direction of the wood grain in the door. A metal door, for example, doesn't have cuts. If you are faux finishing a metal door, you need to create cuts at the "joints"—where a horizontal section connects with a vertical section. Let dry completely.

Apply a second coat, varying the stopping and starting points of the strokes, but still working with the cuts. Curve the strokes slightly for a more natural appearance. Let dry, then apply a third coat.

3. APPLY SECOND GLAZE

Create a slight variation in the wood grain by applying an additional coat using a slightly different color (I used an antique brown tinted glaze like Van Dyke Brown). Let dry thoroughly. There's no need to varnish.

Gallery

Photo courtesy of Anne Soulé, Everett & Soulé

Silver and gold leafing are featured on the stair rail, crown molding and the ceiling in this elegant foyer.

This restaurant showcases several faux finishes. Rub & Run is used on the walls, the ceiling treatment is Old Man Leather and parts of the molding are done in Simple Wood Grain.

All photography courtesy of Anne Soulé, Everett & Soulé

This beautiful dining area displays a ceiling medallion with a Simple Wood Grain finish. The walls are done in Rub & Run.

This home theater features gold leafing on the ceiling and Old Man Leather on the walls. The dentil molding is painted with gold paint and then antiqued with glaze.

Faux Finish Terminology

Aging

Antiqued

Gilding

Aging: The process of making something new or freshly painted look old, well used or weathered.

Antiqued: A process of aging to deepen the tones, adding a richer look.

Cut (in a door): The "cut" in a door is the change of direction of the wood grain, whether it is natural, man-made or imagined.

Distressing: A process of aging in which the surface is purposely worn or damaged. Examples are scratching, denting and chipping paint or causing a finish to amber, as though caused by the weather, use or time.

Drywall Blade: The blade used to smooth joint compound. It has a slight curve in the middle of the blade to allow the compound to be feathered at the edges. Do not use these blades with Venetian plaster, as a drywall blade will not apply the plaster in even coats.

Faux: A French word meaning fake or imitation. It is the art of making something look like something else.

Gilding: Applying metal leaf to a surface so that it appears grander and more expensive.

Glaze: A product that is usually mixed with a color to make the color transparent. There are premixed glazes available or you can use a neutral glaze and mix it with paint. If you are using an oil-based paint, you must use a water-based glaze. The glaze also extends the drying time to allow a longer working time.

Hazardous Products: Check the labels on all products. If it is considered hazardous to the environment, it must be disposed of properly. Check with your city, county or state for regulations.

Joint Compound: The substance used to cover the seams and nail heads when new drywall has been installed. It is the wet compound used to make drywall. It is a substance similar to the look and feel of Venetian plaster, but is not to be confused with Venetian plaster. Joint compound can be used to texture a wall, but it is not very durable.

Rub & Run

Stencil

Venetian Plaster

Lacquer: A clear sealer that is very durable and does not amber when exposed to UV rays. Also used to quicken the drying time for some finishes.

Monochromatic: From "mono" (one) and "chrome" (color), these are paintings that use various values of the same color.

Movement: "Movement" on a wall refers to change in the values of the colors used.

Painter's Tape: This tape is usually blue or lavender. Blue tape can be left on a surface for three days and lavender can be left on a surface for seven days. It is a masking tape with very little tack, so that it can be removed with less chance of leaving a residue or pulling up the surface, whether new paint or paper.

Plaster Blade: The blades used to apply Venetian plaster. They are available in varying widths, usually 2–6 inches (5–15cm).

Polyurethane: A clear sealer that is either sprayed or brushed on to protect a surface. Polyurethane has a tendency to amber, especially in UV rays. It also can be used in a spray form to quicken the drying time for some finishes.

Rub & Run: One of my techniques used for aging surfaces.

Stain: A product used to deepen the color of the surface it is applied to. There are oil-based and water-based stains. Oil-based stain is a penetrating stain, whereas water-based stain is available in either a penetrating or transparent stain. Transparent stain will stay on the surface and does not penetrate, allowing you to work with it and remove as much or as little as needed. Stains can be applied to raw wood to make the wood look like a different type of wood.

Stencil: A pattern that is cut out of either plastic or a thick paper to make multiple copies of the same figures.

Value: The value of a color means nothing more than how dark or light the color is. This can be altered by adding additional coats or by adding white or a touch of black to the paint to lighten or darken the value.

Venetian Plaster: The plaster that is used for several of my faux finishes. Venetian plaster is based on a product that originated in Venice. In Venice, white plaster is primarily used. It is very durable, even with humidity, and is easy to repair.

Resources

PAINT

**Artist's Choice
Saturated Paints**
Sculptural Arts Coating, Inc.
501 Guilford Ave.
Greensboro, NC 27401
800-743-0379
www.sculpturalarts.com

Breakthrough Paints
Star Scenic Supply
4495 S.W. 35th St., Suite D
Orlando, FL 32811
800-485-7827
www.starscenic.com

**Chromatone Quick Dry
Latex Metallics**
Crescent Bronze Powder Co.,
Inc.
3400 N. Avondale Ave.
Chicago, IL 60618
800-445-6810
www.crescentbronze.com

Sherwin-Williams
101 Prospect West
Cleveland, OH 44115
www.sherwinwilliams.com

GLAZES

Golden Artist Colors, Inc.
188 Bell Rd.
New Berlin, NY 13411-9527
800-959-6543
www.goldenpaints.com

Nu-Glaze Glazing Liquid
Star Finishing Products
22 S. Center St.
Hickory, NC 28603-0220
888-STARFIN
www.starfinishing.com

PLASTERS

Kolcaustico Venetian Plaster
Sepp Leaf Products, Inc.
381 Park Ave. S.
New York, NY 10016
800-971-SEPP
www.kolcaustico.com

SmoothRock Pearls & Metals
Briste Group International
North York, Ontario, Canada
M3J 2R8
416-638-6687
www.bristegroup.com

WAXES

**Liberon Black Bison Fine
Paste Wax**
Sepp Leaf Products, Inc.
381 Park Ave. S.
New York, NY 10016
800-971-SEPP
www.kolcaustico.com/liberon.
htm

OTHER MATERIALS

Jacobean Minwax Gel Stain
Minwax Co.
10 Mountainview Rd.

Upper Saddle River, NJ
07458
800-523-9299
www.minwax.com

Krylon Webbing Sprays
800-4KRYLON
www.krylon.com

Rolco Aquasize
Rolco Labs
Carlstad, NJ 07072

Vinyl Cote Flat
T.J. Ronan Paint Corp.
749 E. 135th St.
Bronx, NY 10454
800-247-6626
800-654-3640 (in Texas)
www.ronanpaints.com

Zinsser Bulls Eye Shellac
Zinsser Co., Inc.
173 Belmont Dr.
Somerset, NJ 08875
732-469-8100
www.zinsser.com

Index

The best in home decorating instruction and inspiration is from North Light Books!

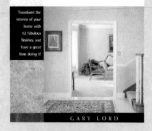

The Art of Trompe L'Oeil Murals

Ideas and inspiration abound in this exquisite book filled with stunning trompe l'oeil work by Yves Lanthier, master muralist. Lanthier has traveled the world in his quest for inspiration and knowledge. He shares his expertise with you in these pages of beautiful photographs filled with examples of his painted rotundas, domes, ceilings, staircases, walls, niches, soffits and doorways. By following the step-by-step illustrations in the book, you can learn to capture the same realistic details found in his lushly painted murals.
ISBN 1-58180-552-7, hard cover with jacket, 128 pages, #33003-K

Elegant Lettering for Your Home

Give your home a refined, personal touch with the simple elegance of hand lettering. This book offers fifteen step-by-step projects that demonstrate a range of applications. You'll learn how to choose an appropriate lettering style, find the center of a surface and arrange lettering to fit the size and shape of any surface. Elegant Lettering for Your Home is all you need to create beautiful home accents!
ISBN 1-58180-578-0, paperback, 128 pages, #33041-K

Pretty Painted Furniture

Now you can add beauty and elegance to every room in your home. Diane Trierweiler makes it easy and fun with step-by-step instructions for giving old furniture a facelift and new furniture a personal touch. Twelve lovely projects teach you how to paint on chests, chairs, tables, armoires and more. It's all the advice and encouragement you need to beautify your furniture with color and style.
ISBN 1-58180-234-X, paperback, 128 pages, #32009-K

Great Paint Finishes for a Gorgeous Home

Gary Lord has been creating beautiful paint finishes professionally for over 20 years. In this book, he shares his tried-and-perfected techniques. Hundreds of full-color photos and friendly instruction make it easy to achieve great, professional looking results. There's also advice on choosing the right colors to make your home gorgeous.
ISBN 0-89134-822-0, hardcover, 128 pages, #31200-K

These books and other fine North Light titles are available at your local arts & craft retailer, bookstore, online supplier or by calling 1-800-448-0915 in North America or 0870 2200220 in the United Kingdom.